The S — — nhouse

A Wisley Handbook

The Small Greenhouse

DEENAGH GOOLD-ADAMS
revised by
RAY WAITE

The Royal Horticultural Society

THE ROYAL HORTICULTURAL SOCIETY

Cassell Educational Limited
Villiers House, 41/47 Strand
London WC2N 5JE
for the Royal Horticultural Society

First published 1974
Second edition 1985
Third edition 1989
Fourth edition 1991

British Library Cataloguing in Publication Data

Goold-Adams, Deenagh
    The small greenhouse — 4th ed.
    1. Greenhouses, Gardening
    I. Title II. Royal Horticultural Society
    III. Series
    635′.0483

    ISBN 0-304-32012-9

Photographs by Michael Warren, Wilf Halliday/RHS and
    the Harry Smith Collection
Typeset by Chapterhouse, Formby
Printed in Hong Kong by Wing King Tong Co. Ltd

Cover: a colourful display of fuchsias and bedding plants with ferns, ivies and pilea
enjoying the more shaded conditions underneath the benches.
    Photograph by Harry Smith Collection
p. 1: a small greenhouse in spring, the benches packed with seedlings.
    Photograph by Michael Warren
p. 2: the climbing *Gloriosa rothschildiana* can be stored as a dry tuber through the winter.
Back cover: hyacinths and *Primula obconica* in a winter greenhouse.
    Photographs by Harry Smith Collection

Contents

Introduction

There is no mystery in the management of a greenhouse. Regular attention and common sense are the basis of all success under glass, while the application of intelligence, ingenuity or expenditure can overcome most problems if time is in short supply! The one essential is a will to grow plants, not just look at them. The key questions are 'Do you want a greenhouse?' and 'Why?'

The greenhouse must give pleasure and fulfil a role, even if this is one that is not recognised by the neighbours or indeed by the family, let alone by any horticultural expert. A greenhouse is a very personal thing and difficult to share, although its maintenance does sometimes demand the cooperation of others.

Today the conservatory has become fashionable as well as useful and is another option. A lean-to greenhouse may be used as a conservatory and is often the cheapest way of extending the home.

To have a small greenhouse is not one of life's major decisions. It is a fringe benefit that may cost more than some wish to spend on a hobby, but it should not cause any more difficulties than buying a freezer or a washing machine.

The fact that every healthy plant grows bigger every day is an everlasting problem. It is sometimes solved by using the greenhouse as a production unit, or as a staging post for plants that will decorate the garden or the home when full grown. There is always an element of this. Some people are only attracted by rare plants whereas others are equally devoted to familiar flowers. Anticipation is probably the keenest pleasure in growing plants, and the increasing skill and knowledge that can be gathered through life is perhaps the greatest satisfaction. Seed sowing and propagation are essential to a lasting interest in a greenhouse and make this form of gardening a good and inexpensive hobby in old age.

As far as pot plants are concerned the greenhouse can be a nursery, a forcing house, a display centre or, alas, a casualty ward and convalescent home. The more knowledgeable and enthusiastic one becomes, the harder it is to limit and rationalise the use of glass; and this often leads to there being not one small

Opposite: the colourful annual *Schizanthus pinnatus* hybrids are easily raised from seed sown in spring or late summer

greenhouse but two or three, when one large one would have been so much easier to manage.

It is a sound idea to start with a mixed collection. In fact it is almost unavoidable; there are many plants so prodigal of seed or easily rooted cuttings that they pass from hand to hand and turn up in most collections.

Although it may seem less than friendly to look a gift-horse in the mouth, it is madness not to examine a gift plant extremely closely before adding it to your collection. A hand lens is helpful for identifying pests, and the tender growing points and the backs of the leaves are the places to look. In any case two weeks isolation is a wise precaution with spraying and fumigation as possible alternatives. In a mixed greenhouse or conservatory one hopes to avoid a serious build-up of the pests that are attracted by any one plant family. There is also more scope for a continuous rather than seasonal display.

The true plantsman who sees each plant individually may not be concerned with the general display at all. The only consideration will be the choice of position of light, shade, warmth and air to suit each treasure best. For there is quite a divergence of microclimates even in small greenhouses. Unhappy plants are worth moving and there should also be no hesitation in examining the roots. It does no harm to knock a plant cleanly out of its pot and replace it, and much can be learnt. Any seriously ailing plant should be discarded completely, unless it is particularly rare or valuable – better by far to make room to grow another specimen to its full potential.

In the very limited space of the small greenhouse or conservatory there is no room to grow a large number of plants perfectly. Indeed half a dozen exhibition plants might fill it. One way to overcome this difficulty is the use of hanging baskets, pots and shelves to create layers of growth.

Another is to concentrate on the 'mini' plant. These have greatly multiplied in recent times, as the need to transport flowering plants by road in cardboard containers hastened the development of compact strains of the most popular plants. Calceolarias, cinerarias, cyclamen, chrysanthemums, gloxinias, saintpaulias and pelargoniums are just some of those that have been induced to concentrate their charms, and together they cover every season. Other plants are naturally small or propagated yearly from small pieces. The enormous and enduring popularity of fuchsias, chrysanthemums and pelargoniums is partly due to the fact that, as they become unmanageably large, they can be replaced by young cuttings taking up much less room.

Another way of saving space is to confine everything to pots too

8

Near-hardy nerines make a fine autumn display in an unheated greenhouse with their lily-like flowers

small for full development. With careful feeding this can be remarkably successful but it does not suit either every plant or every person. Some of us wish to grow the best and discard those that do not meet our high standards.

All greenhouses are much the same in summer, depending only on the management of ventilation, humidity and shading for their differing climates. The key questions for year-long interest are what plants can be over-wintered and how early in the year active growth starts. Many plants have a natural rest at a much lower temperature than for their normal growth, while some, like fuchsias, will either rest or grow according to the temperature. Others will grow in winter and rest in summer if given suitable conditions. Many greenhouse plants come from the southern hemisphere and some can be persuaded that a dry rest in our winter corresponds to the summer drought of their homeland.

The final choice of what to grow will depend on the temperature that is maintained in winter. Without any heat at all the scope for an all-the-year round display is limited by the fact that a plant that is not frost-resistant cannot be guaranteed to survive. All the same a lean-to against a south wall can be very rewarding, and spring comes much earlier under any form of glass.

The so-called 'cold' greenhouse means exactly that and will not

Coleus (left) are excellent foliage plants, though shortlived; *Acacia armata* (right) is one of the best small shrubs for the greenhouse and grows about 10 ft (3m) high

maintain frost-free conditions during really severe weather. However, precautions can be taken to protect hardier plants by using layers of newspaper or sacking. Even then there are limitations on the range of plants that can be over-wintered.

If a minimum winter temperature between 4°C (40°F) and 7°C (45°F) is assured, the greenhouse is usually called 'cool'. This is the most popular form of heated greenhouse. All such greenhouses become easier to manage in winter with every extra degree of heat, although the virtual doubling of the cost of fuel with every extra 2.8°C (5°F) is a powerful deterrent.

Traditionally the cool greenhouse became 'intermediate' when the minimum temperature maintained was 13°C (55°F), but today 'warm' seems a more suitable term and the only question is the definition of warmth. There is a tendency for warmth to begin at 10°C (50°F) in rather the same spirit that life begins at 40! In other words hope springs eternal and some tropical plants will survive although they are happier at 13°C (55°F). This last temperature is the highest that amateurs generally aim at in the free-standing greenhouse. Where there is a conservatory against a house wall connected with the central heating system higher temperatures may prevail and the tropical plants we call house plants can be freely grown.

10

Site and structure

An amateur greenhouse of up to 1000 cubic feet (28m³) does not usually interest the planning authorities, unless it is on a boundary or attached to a building. The local building inspector will have to approve any structure being added to a house and there are regulations about size and use so that it is advisable to check the position locally. If you are a tenant, remember that once fixed to a permanent concrete or brick base, the greenhouse is no longer a tenant's fixture.

Some greenhouses are erected directly on the ground while others have portable base plates of concrete, wood or metal. A really solid base does add to the life of the structure and it is obvious that, if in time the building sags, the glass is likely to crack and leaks will develop. The glass needs to be set in some soft material (putty is no longer used) to avoid leaks and loss of heat in winter.

The materials of which greenhouses are made vary in popularity as their cost and ease of maintenance increase or decrease. It is never difficult to find a possible scientific advantage for either a new or cheaper material. Yet everyone has a preference for wood or metal, regardless of its intrinsic merit, and it is a pity to spend one's leisure in a building one dislikes.

In some settings the traditional white painted softwood is so much more visually satisfying that it must be preferred for a conservatory. Nevertheless the cost of frequent painting needs to be faced. The glazing bars of even a wooden conservatory will probably be of aluminium today.

The most popular wood, known as western red cedar, is a rot-resisting softwood from North America. This wood, from the tree *Thuja plicata*, is usually stained with a solution to make it waterproof and retain the natural red colour. Another method of keeping the wood in good condition is a yearly treatment with thick penetrating oil.

The aluminium alloy greenhouses so popular today need less maintenance than wood, but vary greatly in quality both in design and strength. They can also be had in anodised colour which can have a bronzed appearance or in white vinyl covered aluminium.

Although metal is colder than wood this is not of serious consequence in small lightly constructed buildings. Wood is more convenient when it comes to fixing up shading material or a

11

A traditional wooden greenhouse at the RHS Garden, Wisley

plastic lining. Maximum light in winter is vital, but this is affected more by the position of the greenhouse than its construction nowadays. An east-west orientation is best for winter light but in a very small building this does not make much difference.

A lean-to built against a wall saves some fuel in winter; but it receives less light and is more difficult to ventilate efficiently than the ordinary span-roofed type. A good choice in certain circumstances is a three-quarter span. This over-tops a wall and has two-way ridge ventilation but is an expensive option as it has to be custom-built. A south wall is regarded as the best position, though very hot in summer. Nevertheless, a lean-to on any wall is possible, with a west-facing situation being quite adequate for a wide range of plants during the summer. Sometimes lack of space makes a round or hexagonal greenhouse the best choice.

Transparent films are an alternative to glass. The simplest structure is a walk-in polythene tunnel which, although not particularly attractive, can be used to grow many edible crops and some flowers. There is now available a conventionally styled greenhouse, which has an aluminium structure and is double-glazed with the newer films. It is claimed that these are superior to glass with regard to light transmission. The double glazing is an obvious fuel-saver and also helps to enhance temperatures in a cold greenhouse during spring and autumn, thus extending the growing season.

If a greenhouse is on a solid base, it is less suitable for growing plants in the ground. Brick walls up to the staging save fuel, but are now rare because of the cost of the brickwork. A substantial wooden base is some substitute, but plastic panels do not save fuel unless thick insulating material is fitted inside them. As many additional plants can be grown under the staging when there is glass to the ground, a panelled base can be a false economy.

It is not possible to find all the virtues in one ready-made structure, but it is well worth comparing one with another. The Chelsea and large provincial flower shows are good places to examine a variety of greenhouses and conservatories. As the available site may affect the choice this needs to be considered first. The distance from a source of electricity is important even if it is not going to be used for heating.

Lighting, fans, seed-raisers, mist propagation and power drills are just some of the many extras using electricity. If natural gas is to be used for heating or if an outside oil tank or fuel store will be needed, this is the time to decide where they will be. Mains water is also helpful, even though rain water is often preferred to tap water. Automatic watering may need mains water pressure or a water tank at least 3 ft (90cm) above the staging.

If plants are to be grown in the ground, the soil must be fairly

An aluminium greenhouse at the Chelsea Show

A greenhouse at Wisley with an aluminium frame covered in transparent film

well drained and this is more easily attended to before the greenhouse is put up.

A position that is open to winter sunlight and not overshadowed by trees or buildings is the aim, and one does not want a hedge or fence too close although shelter from wind is important. There is some conflict of opinion as to which way to align the greenhouse, though this may be determined by the site. For the small greenhouse, alignment is not that critical, but I favour a north-south orientation.

Here are some points to look for when choosing a small greenhouse or conservatory:

1. Method and amount of ventilation and whether it can be automated. Extra ventilation is almost always essential as when the ventilators are open they should equal at least one fifth of the floor area and ideally open to an angle of 50°.
2. General stability and likely wind resistance if the site is exposed.
3. Foundations required and method of construction.
4. Strength and height of staging provided and whether it is suitable for your purposes. Much gravel, clay pots or sand capillary benches can be heavy. One needs an absolutely flat surface for all capillary watering.
5. Removal of excess condensation. Make sure there is an adequate channel on the glazing bars to achieve this.
6. Width of entrance and height of sill. Also ensure that the door has strong fixings and opens easily.
7. Check terms if manufacturers deliver and erect, and look at 'Do it yourself' building instructions.
8. Make sure glass and base plate are included in the price and discover if they will be delivered with the greenhouse.

If a greenhouse is put up on grass, the turf should be removed with an inch of top soil and stacked to make potting soil. However, the busy gardener may feel more inclined to cover the grass with black plastic sheeting until it is dead and then cultivate the soil or remove it for use elsewhere. If plants are grown in the ground, the soil is managed much as in the open garden, bearing in mind that it does not have the benefit of frost or rain. A friable loam containing plenty of organic matter is the aim.

When ground is not cultivated, the floor inside the greenhouse can be treated in various ways. On a wet site concrete is probably the best. For retaining moisture in summer, when the floor is sprayed to increase the humidity, rammed soil or ash with a duck-board path has been the traditional working arrangement. A central path of paving blocks with gravel on the soil under the benches is more attractive. A conservatory often looks best if the same paving as the terrace continues inside or alternatively if the flooring in the house is carried through to the conservatory. This is not always practical. Wall to wall carpeting cannot be 'damped down' and vinyl tiles can be death traps when wet. Where a solid floor is constructed insulation with polystyrene sheeting can be of value, since 8 per cent of heat is lost downwards.

The actual foundations of a free-standing greenhouse should rest on firm sub-soil. When laying concrete or brick foundations, leave entry points for electric cables and water pipes. Pieces of hose do well for this, although I once found that a pygmy vole took up residence as a result!

A greenhouse is really incomplete without a cold frame. This is an intermediate stage for hardening off plants before planting them outside. Alternatively plants can be grown in the frame before bringing them in to frost-free conditions.

A cold frame is essential if one is to make the most of a greenhouse

Heating, ventilation and shading

HEATING

The cost of heating has multiplied so many times in recent years that we hesitate before deciding to heat a greenhouse at all. At the same time the savings made by raising, preserving and propagating our own plants have also greatly increased.

An amateur's collection of plants can be irreplaceable, costly to replace, or almost valueless; so the cost of installing and running an efficient heating system during a severe winter may be either well worthwhile or quite unacceptable.

A cold greenhouse will only protect hardy plants from wind and rain, but this is not usually the aim. Most of us have a mixture of tender plants and want some to be decorative at all seasons. This is even more true of a conservatory attached to the house. Few plants mind a brief drop in temperature so long as they do not freeze, especially if this happens during a fairly dormant growth period.

The cost of heating will vary with the region of the country and elevation of the site. Exposure, too, is an important factor, for heat loss can double with winds blowing at 15 mph (24 kmph). Insulation will of course help, but it must be as complete as possible for maximum effect. Various transparent films which provide double glazing have become popular, especially now that plastic studs and other fixings are obtainable for aluminium greenhouses. Bubble plastic is particularly efficient and, although it reduces light transmission, this is unlikely to be detrimental to the normal range of plants grown. Plastic film also is a convenient material for partitioning a greenhouse, so that only a small area needs to be heated. Taking this a stage further, a propagating frame will give very comfortable conditions for small plants.

A simple calculation can be used to gain a fairly accurate idea of the heat required to keep temperatures at an acceptable level. No allowance need be made for the differences in heat loss through various materials. First, measure the total surface area of roof, sides and floor, including any small walls and doors. Secondly, decide on the temperature lift required. This is the difference between the lowest temperature likely to be experienced in a given area and the minimum temperature necessary for the plants concerned. With this information, calculate thus:

Area in square feet × temperature lift in °F × 1.4 = Btu/hour

or

$$\frac{\text{Area in metres}^2 \times \text{temperature lift in °C} \times 7.9}{1000} = \text{kWatt}$$

(3412 Btu = 1 kWatt)

The resultant figure, rounded up, will give the output required from a given heat source.

Greenhouses can be heated by natural or bottled gas, solid fuel, paraffin or electricity. The latter is now the cheapest when fan heaters are used.

Natural gas heaters can be vory good, but as with the simple paraffin types, the greenhouse should be slightly ventilated at all times so that any injurious gases and excess condensation can be dissipated. Gas heaters can usually be modified to burn bottled gas. Thermostatic control is not available on all models and even then most rely on non-electric operation.

Electric heaters should always be fitted with a thermostat. To give accurate control, the thermostat should be aspirated and sited in the centre of the greenhouse. However, small fan heaters usually have the thermostat incorporated in the unit itself. A recent survey has shown that electric tubular heaters are not very economical in terms either of initial outlay or running costs.

There is no doubt that traditional hot water pipes are still the best for a larger greenhouse, particularly if it is joined to the house, when the central heating system can be extended. A free-standing separate boiler requires more attention, especially if solid fuel is used. Oil and gas as heat sources can be very convenient and automatically controlled.

Whatever the system, there will always be cold and warm spots, although these can be used to advantage. A maximum and minimum thermometer will record what is actually happening in various positions. Different temperature zones will be very noticeable with gas or paraffin heaters, while electric fan heaters tend to give more even heat distribution.

VENTILATION

Heating is only part of the control of climate under glass and to create good growing conditions it is also necessary to adjust to the prevailing weather. Even in midwinter during a cold spell, sun shining on glass can raise the temperature appreciably and as the season progresses heat can become excessive. The trapped

17

warmth does not escape as quickly as it is gained, so ventilation may be necessary at any time. Rapid fluctuations in temperature should always be guarded against, but this is much more difficult in small greenhouses where the volume of air is not large. For a few people with leisure, it may be a pleasure to keep a constant eye on the weather and wind direction, so that greenhouse ventilation can be adjusted accordingly. For most gardeners, this is impractical, but it is possible to reach some sort of compromise. In any case, it is much better to give more ventilation when leaving for the day in spring, summer and autumn, even if temperatures go down somewhat.

Simple automatic ventilator openers can be fitted. These consist of a cylinder filled with a waxy substance that expands and contracts with the temperature and in turn moves a piston up and down, thus opening and closing the ventilators. They can be sluggish in action but are a good first line of defence and need not be fitted to every opening. Much more sophisticated electrically operated equipment is also available.

Extractor fans are useful. They should be sited away from the door and, as they are thermostatically controlled, should be set to operate at a few degrees above the thermostat setting for the heating.

It is a great mistake to allow temperatures to rise excessively before ventilating; far better to anticipate the situation and ventilate early. Ventilation at the greenhouse ridge should in fact open up an area not less then one fifth of the floor area, so it will be readily appreciated that most small greenhouses as bought off the shelf are under-ventilated. If such a purchase is being considered, always ensure that extra ventilators can be obtained. Side ventilators are also important and become less obtrusive when fitted as louvres. Automatic openers are also available for these.

SHADING

Shade is another way of lowering temperatures under glass, and may be required as early as March for shade-loving plants and small seedlings. A high proportion of greenhouse plants benefit from some shading from April until the end of September. It is, of course, only actually wanted when the sun is shining, but it is usual to compromise and create a filtered light that is not too dark on dull days.

Shading on the outside of the greenhouse is the most efficient in terms of lowering temperature and blinds that can be raised and lowered are the ideal. It is possible to have automatic control, but

Primula malacoides, a delightful winter-flowerer for the cool greenhouse

this is particularly expensive. Internal blinds of green-tinted plastic sheeting work reasonably well. An alternative is a white wash shading painted on the glass, which is quite satisfactory, and there is a proprietary product that becomes fairly translucent in dull wet weather. Fine plastic netting designed to give various degrees of shading is also available and, when fixed on a length of wood, can be rolled across the greenhouse roof as required.

The other means of combating excessive heat in summer is by increasing the humidity, damping down paths, benches and even walls. Evaporation has a cooling effect and also helps to create a growing atmosphere. This is discussed in the next chapter.

Watering and humidity

WATERING

Watering in the greenhouse is an essential activity about which there is much disagreement. Some plants prefer a constant moisture, while others are believed to prefer to become rather dry before being watered. In practice the majority will adapt fairly readily to any steady regime that does not keep them sodden or allow them to dry out enough to begin to wilt. It is, however, a golden rule when watering by hand either to give enough water to moisten all the soil in the pot or to refrain from watering at all. Clean rain water (except in very large industrial towns) is likely to be better for the more delicate pot plants and may be essential for lime-hating plants if the mains water is very alkaline. It is also an advantage if water can stand in the greenhouse before use in cold weather to take the chill off. However, tap water coming under pressure is highly charged with oxygen which is beneficial and static tanks easily become polluted. It is not always understood that air penetrates between the soil particles and that it is essential to all but bog plants that it should. If water fills all the air spaces in the soil for long, most plants will suffer root damage.

Every beginner wants to know how often to water in terms of days and this is an unanswerable question. The rate at which the soil in a pot dries out is affected by sunshine, temperature, atmospheric moisture, type of compost, and how firmly it is packed. The nature and size of the plants and whether they are growing or resting are other factors, not to mention the material of which the pot is made. The advantage of hand watering is that it can be selective, and success must be based on observation.

Holidays and other absences from home are the bane of the greenhouse enthusiast, and now that automatic watering is so widely practised commercially every amateur should give it serious thought.

There are two main types of watering system that can be fully automated. The first is capillary watering, by which pots standing on damp (capillary) matting or sand draw water from below by capillary attraction. The second method is to water the surface of the soil in each pot by means of an individual nozzle or tube. Such trickle and drip systems need electricity for true automation, whereas capillary systems need only a source of water.

The florists' cyclamen, derived from *C. persicum*, is available in many different colours

It is difficult to give simple general advice about automatic watering, because conditions in each greenhouse and the collection of plants grown vary enormously. Even when a watering method is chosen, the interests and aptitudes of the gardener will affect the result, as in all gardening. Temperatures maintained in winter and the method of heating will also alter the climatic conditions in which the watering takes place. Nevertheless, a general understanding of the principles involved and the equipment available is essential, if the best use is to be made of it.

Those specialising in a single kind of plant or crop are faced with the limited problem of its season of growth and rest, but most amateurs grow a mixed collection of plants in pots as well as raising seedlings in spring.

The average small greenhouse tends to be too hot in summer, poorly ventilated, and with too dry an atmosphere. All forms of automatic watering are likely to improve these conditions, and capillary benches, which add moisture to the air and accommodate the largest number of plants in the smallest area, are particularly suitable.

In winter the problems are different. In many greenhouses a combination of low temperatures with a damp atmosphere and poor air circulation encourages troubles such as botrytis, and unnecessary dampness is to be avoided. As better air circulation is achieved with slatted benches, it would be ideal if each pot stood well clear of its neighbours and was watered individually according to its needs.

Capillary watering

The capillary bench is in many ways the most easily controlled and satisfactory method of automatic watering. A sand bench is constructed where the pots stand on damp sand which is 2 in. (5 cm) above the water-level. The valuable aspect of this system is that each pot plant standing on damp sand absorbs from below, by capillary attraction, only the amount of water it uses. So long as the bench has a controlled and constant water level, sudden changes in the weather and the water needs of the plants are catered for. As there is never a shortage of water, the plants grow steadily and fast.

There is a limit to the height of the pot that can be used when watering by this method. The capillary attraction only carries the water up about 5 in. (12.5cm) when the water level is held 1.5 to 2 in. (5cm) below the surface of the sand, which has been found to be the most satisfactory arrangement for most plants. Pots up to 6 in. (15cm) high are satisfactory on capillary benches; larger pots are better watered from the top. For a really reliable and effective capillary bench, it is necessary for it to be level ($\pm \frac{1}{8}$ in.; 3 mm) and to have a controlled, constant water level. It is possible to cover capillary benches with plastic sheeting with a hole for each pot if one is seriously concerned to reduce atmospheric humidity, but I have never found any need for this. Plants that need to be kept dry when resting are, of course, removed from the bench.

On all forms of capillary bench there must be direct contact between the damp surface of the bench and the compost in the pots. This means that there is no drainage material in the bottom of the pots. Modern plastic pots do not need this anyway. If clay pots are used, a small piece of glass-fibre insulating material can be inserted into the drainage hole to act as a wick. To establish capillarity, pots put on the bench are pressed firmly on to the sand with a slight twisting action. In hot weather if there is any doubt whether capillarity has been achieved, water once from above.

The compost used on all kinds of capillary bench must be well aerated if the plants are to thrive. This means that all potting is done very lightly – just a tap on the bench and a very light firming with the fingers around the edge when re-potting, but no hard ramming. The expert grower of exhibition plants may complain that this is not the way to grow a fine hardwooded plant, and he

Gerbera jamesonii 'Happipot', a dwarf seed strain which is ideal for the small greenhouse

may be right. All I can say is that a mass of healthy and attractive plants can be grown with ease and success. Opinions differ as to what modifications to make to the compost for plants on capillary benches. I use John Innes composts with a little additional coarse grit or sand. I have also used soilless composts and mixtures of peat and loam-based compost. The one essential is to avoid consolidating the compost and to re-pot if a plant looks sickly for no apparent reason. It is wise to keep newly potted plants off the bench for two or three days, as those with damaged roots do not take kindly to this form of watering.

For a home-made capillary bench all that is required is a level bench that is strong enough to support 2 in. (5cm) of wet sand and the pots without sagging. A solid edge to the staging is also desirable, and the whole is made waterproof with a single sheet of medium or heavy quality plastic sheeting.

The capillary watering kits sold to amateurs are usually designed for use with capillary matting and many are only used at holiday time. Capillary matting is rather ugly and needs fairly frequent renewal, but it can be made to work well. It is essential to test the system thoroughly before a holiday as, if things go wrong, the matting dries very quickly.

The water level can be controlled in various ways. The ordinary domestic ball-cock is a rather rough instrument for making a sensitive response to very small demands for water. There are small plastic floats as used in the self-filling individual drinking bowls designed for cattle. These do not need mains water pressure to work and the amateur plumber can fit them up. If benches are of differing heights, each level will need a separate water control consisting of one of these floats in a plastic box with a plastic tube from the water supply and another to the bottom of the bench. A tiny hole can be made in the plastic sheeting at the base of the bench and small black plastic tubing pushed gently through it, to give a waterproof joint.

Do not use transparent plastic piping as algae will grow inside it and block it in hot weather. Light coloured tanks are also a mistake. Algae will also grow on the matting. This does not matter but is ugly. The matting can be washed or treated with chemicals.

In time algae and moss will grow on the sand, and chemicals are sometimes used to prevent this. I prefer to scrape off and re-place the surface of the sand occasionally and one can also wash and replace all the sand. Obtaining coarse sand in quantities of more than 7 lb (3kg) and less than a lorry load is the main difficulty with this system.

With capillary watering, no matter what equipment is used, one does want to be able to see at a glance whether the apparatus is working. When buying any automated equipment always ask the question: 'How do I see instantly if it has stopped working?'

If it is impossible to achieve a really level surface, one can have an irrigated capillary bench. This consists of a sand-covered bench which is kept watered but is not waterproof at the edges, so that surplus water drains away. A capillary mat can also be used in this way. It is merely a way of adding to the humidity and lessening the individual watering. Capillarity is easily lost in hot weather and it does not have the reliability or usefulness of the controlled capillary bench.

Point watering

There are a number of watering systems that bring water to each plant, either trickling out of adjustable nozzles or dripping from fine tubing. With these the plants may be potted in the traditional ways and the pots can stand on any freely draining staging. Trickle lines and seep-hose can also be used to water plants growing in the ground and to keep irrigated benches moist. When used on the ground a point to remember is that, although long periods of watering penetrate more deeply, a wider area of soil is dampened by more frequent watering for shorter periods.

The pendent flowers of *Kalanchoe manginii* look best in a hanging basket

There is a variety of drip-watering arrangements using very small-bore plastic tubing with individual tubes to each pot; these are supplied by larger-bore rigid tubing. They can have adjustable rates of drip for different plants and positions, and can be tailored to suit any pot arrangement, although an artistic arrangement of plants is made more difficult. With fine tubing the trouble to watch for is blockage of small tubes from lime in the water. These systems are often activated by turning on a tap for a time each day. To automate drip systems, high-pressure water and also electricity are desirable, but amateur kits are available using a simple syphon system. In these, water drips slowly into a small tank, which, when full, empties through the trickle or drip lines connected to it. The disadvantage of this system is that a slow drip, if left unattended for long, is apt to stop completely, while a rapid drip will give too much water.

A sophisticated system using an electric solar control, which adjusts the watering according to the weather, is available for controlling either watering or mist propagation but this is a costly solution.

Perhaps the most obvious way to water plants automatically is to imitate rain, and this is done through nozzles of a similar type to those used for mist propagation. All effective systems of this kind need a source of water at mains pressure or a special pump. In hard water districts continual spraying will leave an ugly lime deposit on both plants and greenhouse glass which is difficult to remove. Where plants needing high humidity are grown, automatic spraying may be used for damping down the floor.

Those who want to specialise in lime-hating plants in districts with very alkaline water must remember that, unless they have ample supplies of rain water, or are prepared for the considerable cost of treating the water, their plants may suffer on an automated watering system.

Electric watering systems

The more elaborate automatic watering schemes use electricity. If both water and electricity are available, there is virtually no watering problem that cannot be solved at a price. The simplest arrangement that works reliably in one's own circumstances is usually the best. One thing to bear in mind is that there is no equipment for controlling the flow of water on a small scale which it is beyond the wit of ordinary people to understand. What is happening may be boxed in or obscured by technical terms, but it is bound to be based on some fairly simple principle. This can be understood and will be explained to those determined to know. Watering arrangements once installed must remain in working order for long periods, and it is virtually impossible to keep equipment working continuously if one does not understand it. Before installing anything that might need professional servicing, it is wise to check whether this is available as well as its likely cost.

Several methods of adjusting the frequency of watering to the weather have been used with varying success. A time clock can be altered to match the season and can operate on a less than daily basis in winter, but it takes no account of whether the sun is shining or not. A solar control using a photo-electric cell has been used with success for some years. It needs to be fixed facing due south and is then activated by the amount of light falling on it. This does not necessarily match up precisely to the amount of water needed, but it is adjustable.

To turn water on and off solenoid (magnetic) valves have long been used, together with a time clock or other electronic controller. A daily watering of not less than 15 or 20 minutes can be arranged by using an ordinary time clock (as used in domestic central heating systems) together with a solenoid valve. If a very short watering time is needed, it becomes more complicated and expensive because a second time clock is necessary. The first (24

Calceolarias growing in the glasshouses at Wisley

hour) time clock is set to come on for 1 hour a day and to switch on
a second (1 hour) time clock which may be set for as little as 2 or 3
minutes. All this can work off mains electricity, but as it is considered safer in greenhouses to use low voltages, the electronic
controllers designed for horticultural use usually have a trans-
former and work at 24 volts. These are linked to low-voltage
solenoid valves. It is possible to have solenoids for all the various
couplings of high and low voltage and water pressure, but one
must be sure of what is needed. Obviously it is possible to bring
the silicon chip into play and the day may come when the
gardener presses a few keys by the bedside to activate all systems.

HUMIDITY

Many of us as children have watched the sluicing down of paths
and the spraying of foliage in some large public or private greenhouse. Indeed the warm green smell of damp soil and the mingled
scents of growing plants is what the words greenhouse and conservatory conjure up in our minds. This is the good growing
atmosphere gardeners talk about. The amount of moisture in the
air, and hence coolness in warm weather, is much influenced by
the amount of green growth within the greenhouse. If there is a

27

concrete floor and a few rather dry pot plants, the temperature will rise very rapidly and the air will be far too dry.

Many gardeners are able and willing to water by hand, using either a watering can or hose. The best can is one with a long spout to facilitate reaching between plants. Hoses may be fitted with trigger-controlled lances and these too make for ease of operation.

The lavish use of hoses is hardly appropriate in the small greenhouse, but in summer there is a great need to increase the humidity in the air as well as to cool it. Some compromise needs to be made between what is desirable and what is practical. Spraying the floor morning and evening in the summer months is one way out, but the effect is not lasting in hot sunny weather and a more frequent automated spraying would be better. For many plants, shade as well as humidity will be necessary, particularly if the ventilation is poor.

From October to March no extra dampness is needed, and in cool conditions the less water that is splashed about the better. In winter, hand watering should be done early in the day. The human senses are adept at judging atmospheric humidity once they know what is wanted. People tend to feel uncomfortable when the humidity falls below 50%, and this is too dry for plants. A daytime atmospheric humidity around 60 to 65% seems to be satisfactory for most plants. The humidity at night will be and should be higher.

Although mist propagation is not strictly what is meant by watering, I mention it here because it is a useful tool for those who have to be away a great deal. As well as rooting the more difficult cuttings, seeds can be raised to the pricking out stage under mist, and the plants then put on capillary benches.

In mist propagation various forms of so-called 'electronic leaf' are used to control the amount of misting. Perhaps the simplest of these is the one directly linked with the actual conditions of humidity. In this the weight of water falling as mist turns off the system, until the plastic foam sponge which has absorbed the water dries out enough to alter a weight balance and thus turns on the mist once more. The other electronic leaves depend on water connecting electrodes and then breaking the current as they dry out. These may need frequent cleaning if the water is limy. A good alternative is the solar control already described.

Soils and feeding

SOILS

A simple way to start growing pot plants is to buy a bag of ready-made compost and use it straight from the bag. Today, the choice is bewildering and ever changing, as the combination of research and marketing soon establishes new composts if they prove useful in nursery practice. These are mainly for the production of young plants, which is also what many amateurs are engaged in. However, the more permanent or specimen pot plant still responds to a traditional diet and each one of us will adhere to methods found successful in our own conditions.

Good John Innes compost is as good as it ever was, but unfortunately it becomes rarer every day. The composts are based on a medium loam soil, which only exists in a limited area of the country and is in very short supply. Before being used for potting, turves from good pasture are supposed to be stacked for some months with an even scarcer commodity, strawy manure, and then the whole heap mixed together and screened before being sterilised. Quite apart from the labour involved, the cost of transporting such heavy materials from one part of the country to another has become uneconomic. The result is that much of the John Innes compost sold is made with unsuitable soil. It may also be difficult to find suitable loam to make up one's own compost. However, if the soil is going to be less than ideal anyway, the home-made compost may be preferable for those who have the time and inclination to prepare it.

The loam should pass through a $\frac{3}{8}$ in. (6–7mm) sieve and must be sterilised. This means bringing it up to a temperature of $82\,^{\circ}$C ($180\,^{\circ}$F) and maintaining it there for twenty minutes either in a special steriliser or a saucepan over hot water.

To make John Innes seed compost, 2 parts loam, 1 part granulated peat and 1 part coarse sand (all by bulk) are mixed together, with the addition of $1\frac{1}{2}$ oz (40g) superphosphate of lime and $\frac{3}{4}$ oz (20g) of either finely ground chalk or limestone. These ingredients need thorough mixing.

The proportions for making John Innes potting composts are 7 parts loam, 3 parts peat and 2 parts sand. To this is added 4 oz (115g) John Innes Base Fertilizer per bushel for the No. 1 compost, 8 oz (225g) per bushel for No. 2, and 12 oz (340g) for No. 3. Ground chalk or limestone is also added to the potting soils at the rate of $\frac{3}{4}$ oz (20g) per bushel for No. 1 compost (for very young plants), $1\frac{1}{2}$ oz (40g) for the No. 2 compost (for most plants), and 3 oz (85g) for the No. 3 compost (which is needed for strong growing plants in large pots or tubs).

There are now some ready-made composts which are of the John Innes type but use modern slow-release fertilizers. These are sometimes in a separate sachet which enables the compost to be stored for longer without deteriorating. All loam-based composts are best used fresh. Another development is the substitution of perlite for the coarse grit or sand in the traditional mixtures. This may not be better but is certainly lighter in weight, which can be important.

A point the manufacturers seem to have overlooked is that keen gardeners like to experiment and mix their own composts. This may upset the scientist's careful formulae, but many amateurs mix ready-made soil-based and soilless composts together. A half and half mixture is popular and goes some way towards correcting the tendency of plants in peat to become top-heavy.

During the last twenty years there has been a steady increase in the use of peat-based composts. A peat and vermiculite mixture is also used, and more recently the all-peat and perlite composts have been developed. None of these have to be sterilised and they can be stored without changing their character, unlike soil.

It is an advantage of the manufactured composts, or substrates

Mixed tuberous begonias on a greenhouse bench

Spring bulbs like *Iris reticulata* and *Narcissus* 'Tête-à-Tête' will flower earlier in a cold greenhouse

as they are sometimes called, that they are lighter in weight and more uniform than anything containing soil. Nevertheless, they are not suitable for large specimen plants and the watering technique is different from that in soil-based composts. Peat holds more water than soil but dries out more quickly, and once dry may be difficult to wet. All the same most bought pot plants are in some type of peat compost and their care is familiar to many. As the distribution of the various composts is not evenly spread over the country, amateurs need to become accustomed to one or more that are readily available locally. Pine bark and plastic waste are other materials used in some composts.

It is important to remember that plants grown in soilless composts need supplementary feeding sooner than those grown in soil-based composts, as they do not have the natural reserve of plant nutrients found in soil. The modern slow-release and chelated fertilizers are suited to peat and sand composts and have often been included in their composition.

A potting shed can be regarded either as a necessity or a luxury depending on circumstances; but obviously it is undesirable to store composts, fertilizers, pesticides or unwashed pots in the

Hippeastrum 'Apple Blossom' is one of several named forms of the very popular "amaryllis"

greenhouse. Where there are children, a locked cupboard for pesticides and herbicides, away from heat, frost or food, is much more important than a potting shed.

The basic ingredients of all potting composts have been loam, sand, leafmould and well-rotted manure. Each of these is a variable substance, and it is only with experience that one comes to know the feel of a compost that is porous and open, and yet with sufficient humus to retain moisture and nutrition and to support healthy growth. Both the plants grown and the watering methods determine the most effective compost.

Loam. Fibrous loam, the basis of all traditional potting mixtures, is not just garden soil but the top 4 or 5 in. (10–12.5cm) of well grazed pasture, which has been stacked for a year until the grass has rotted, leaving the fibrous soil. For making John Innes composts it is suggested that a 2 in. (5cm) layer of manure should be spread on every second layer of turves with a sprinkling of ground limestone on the alternate layers. The whole heap should be thoroughly wet right through and then be protected from heavy rain and left to rot down.

Leafmould. This vital ingredient went out of fashion and was replaced by peat; nevertheless the most dedicated gardeners have never abandoned leafmould if they have a source of supply. It is the product of the decay of leaves of deciduous trees, preferably beech and oak. If collected in autumn and turned once or twice, they break down in about eighteen months into a light fluffy substance that can be passed through a ½ in. (1cm) sieve. If just left lying in a wired enclosure, leaves usually take two years to decay sufficiently. It must be remembered that there will be lime in leafmould from trees on limy soil. Lime-free leafmould is a useful potting material for lime-hating and shrubby plants.

Peat. For potting composts granular sphagnum is best. Peat does not contain plant food.

Sand. Sand should be coarse, clean and lime-free. Soft yellow builder's sand is not suitable for potting, nor is sea sand unless very thoroughly washed to remove salt. The sand particles should be up to ⅛ in. size (3mm).

Vermiculite. This substance is extremely light and absorbent. In a granulated form mixed with peat and fertilizers it forms one of the commercial composts. It is also available as a sterile medium without nutrients. Cuttings can be rooted in it or in a mixture of peat and vermiculite. It is so light that young plants can be lifted from it without damaging the finest roots.

Streptosolen jamesonii, a semi-climbing shrub which does not get out of hand, is ideal for a small conservatory

Perlite. This is also a light and absorbent substance created by the heat treatment of volcanic rock. It can be used in a similar manner to vermiculite and is also used in orchid composts, sometimes being substituted for the grit or sand in John Innes type composts. It is available in a variety of granule sizes for different purposes.

Wood ashes. These should be kept dry until used. They are an organic source of potash and are sometimes added to composts, particularly if the soil is heavy.

Lime. Lime is not a fertilizer in the usual sense, although it supplies calcium which many plants need. It improves the texture of clay soils and corrects acidity, but it should not be applied to soil with a pH of 6.5 or above, (pH is a measure of acidity). The neutral point is pH 7.0. Above is alkaline and below acid. A pH of 6.3 is considered best for John Innes compost and pH 5.3 to 5.5 for peat and sand composts. For lime-hating plants the pH needs to be below 6.0. One can discover the pH of the soil with a simple soil testing outift. One can also ignore the whole thing and hope it is all right!

Manure. Cow manure is perhaps the most generally satisfactory for horticultural purposes, if obtainable, but horse manure is good for heating up a slow compost heap. Poultry manure is chemically rich unless it has been spoilt by exposure to the weather. It should be stored dry under cover. No manure should be used in a greenhouse border until it is in a well-rotted state.

Fish meal. This is an organic source of nitrogen, phosphorus and potash and is a useful fertilizer for the greenhouse border.

Bonemeal. This slow-acting fertilizer, containing phosphorus and a little nitrogen, suffered an eclipse owing to the fear of its transmitting disease, but is now always heat treated.

FEEDING

When plants are growing strongly and the pots are full of roots, the question of additional feeding arises. Some understanding of the processes of plant growth is helpful. We all realise that air, water, light and sufficient warmth must be supplied for growth to take place. Then the leaves will be able to manufacture sugars, starches and proteins, while the roots obtain the various essential minerals and moisture from the soil. Nitrogen, phosphates and potassium, sometimes cryptically referred to as NPK, are the most used and most likely to need replacement. They are present in

Part of the glasshouse complex at Wisley

various proportions in all the compound fertilizers and liquid feeds. Those designed for foliage plants will have more nitrogen, whereas those intended for quick growing flowering plants will have more phosphates and those for tomatoes more potassium. A tomato fertilizer is a convenient source of potash for the occasional feeding of most plants. A frequent error of amateurs is to confine themselves to one liquid feed meant for foliage house plants and then to be amazed when flowering is disappointing.

The precise and detailed needs of many plants are not known, and until recently the essential trace elements found in natural soils could not be included in fertilizers or composts. Now the dedicated gardener can use slow-release fertilizers and many trace elements fused into microscopic glass pellets, and these are even to be found in some commercial composts. Another possibility is the foliar feed whereby plants absorb nutrients through their leaves when sprayed with the diluted feed. This is a quick pick-me-up when things have gone wrong and a sickly plant whose root action is not good can often be encouraged to grow away strongly by foliar feeding.

The secret of feeding is to give little and often and never more than is suggested on the packet. Plants that are resting do not need feeding.

Plants from seed

Sowing tiny seeds and watching the whole process develop, no matter how long it takes, is a never-ending pleasure to those who become deeply involved in gardening. At the same time there is nothing more maddening than careful sowing, a long wait, and then no results. Many of us will never attempt to acquire the right mental attitude to raise rare shrubs or difficult alpines from seed. But there is room for all tastes in the greenhouse and a wide variety of reliable seeds will give rapid and predictable results with reasonable care. Some plants regarded as difficult are in fact easy, if one can sow fresher seed than is often available in a packet. The length of time seed remains viable is extremely varied and greatly affected by the way it is kept. Although one is advised not to discard pans of rare seeds for two or three years, this is unpractical and depressing in the average small greenhouse.

The equipment used for seed sowing under glass ranges from the fast disappearing clay seed pan and wooden box through plastic trays, pots and pans to peat pots and compressed soil blocks as well as the plastic cast-offs of modern living. Every amateur evolves a personal method, but all successful arrangements ensure a temperature sufficient to allow germination and moisture that is constant without being excessive. It is sometimes said that the ideal temperature for germination of seeds is 5.6°C (10°F) above the optimum growing temperature of the plant concerned. This is only a very rough guide and one cannot give each packet of seed a different temperature. As 21°C (70°F) is satisfactory for the germination of a great many seeds of greenhouse and bedding plants, most seed raisers are designed to raise the temperature to this level. The simpler types lift the temperature but do not have thermostatic control, so that one must guard against the sun shining on them. The most elaborate kinds with both soil and air heating on separate thermostats are very costly. However, soil warming cables can be put into benches or frames and there are many ways of arranging a warm corner in a cooler greenhouse. The highest temperature is only required until the seeds germinate. All seeds need to be sown much more thinly than comes naturally, with the smallest ones merely pressed lightly into the surface and the larger ones buried to their own depth in the compost.

The traditional way of covering seed boxes is a sheet of glass

Abutilon hybrids (left) may be raised from seed or cuttings; *Campanula fragilis* (right) is very similar to the better-known *C. isophylla*

and a sheet of brown paper or newspaper. However, the glass has to be turned each day to remove condensation. An alternative covering is black polythene or milky bubble plastic sheeting or, better still, several layers of hessian or similar material, which should be kept well moistened. Many seed-raisers have stiff plastic covers and only need shading from sunlight. No matter how the seeds are covered, daily inspection is advisable since they must have good light as soon as they germinate. A few plants, including *Primula obconica* and *P. sinensis*, germinate best in light and some do so only in the dark.

Choose a container for sowing in commensurate in size with the quantity of seed available and the number of seedlings required. Too large a receptacle is wasteful of space in a seed-raiser or on a greenhouse bench and uses unnecessary compost. The moment any seedlings appear, they should be moved to stronger light and cooler conditions. They must never dry out or be allowed to stop growing; therefore early pricking out is usually advised. This is always a matter of judgement if the weather is bad and the temperature low, but crowding does weaken growth.

Most plants are pricked out into larger, deeper trays about 2 in. (5cm) apart in a slightly richer compost. These are easier to keep evenly moist by hand watering than individual small pots. However, if one does not want enough plants to fill the boxes, individual plastic pots may be better, particularly on capillary benches. Quantities of seedlings urgently needing pricking out at the same moment are one of the nightmares of gardening.

Overleaf are some suggestions for plants to grow from seed for greenhouse decoration with sowing dates and the approximate time taken to flower.

37

Table: plants from seed (A = annual, B = biennial, P = perennial; MWT = minimum winter temperature)

Name	Sowing date; time taken to flower; MWT
Abutilon x *hybridum*. P.	Spring 16 weeks. 7°C (45°F). (See p. 37.)
Alonsoa warscewiczii. P, grown as A.	March to May. 16 weeks.
Asparagus densiflorus 'Myers' (*A. myersii*) and 'Sprengeri' (*A. sprengeri*). P.	Spring. Foliage plants. 7°C (45°F).
Begonia semperflorens. P.	February or March. 6 months. 10°C (50°F).
Browallia speciosa. P.	March or June. 6 months. 10°C (50°F) for winter flowers.
Calceolaria. A and P.	June for flowering following spring. MWT 7°C (45°F). (See p. 27.)
Campanula fragilis and *C. isophylla* P. Trailing.	Spring. 16 weeks. 4°C (40°F). (See p. 37.)
Celosia cristata. A.	March. 20 weeks.
Cineraria. See *Senecio*.	
Coleus. P, grown as A.	Early spring in heat. Foliage plant. Discard autumn. (See p. 10.)
Cuphea. A and P.	March. 16 weeks. 7°C (45°F).
Cyclamen. P.	June to August. 15 or 16 months. 7°C (45°F). Also F₁ hybrids from March sowing to flower November onwards. (See p. 21.)
Didiscus caerulea. A.	Spring. 18 weeks.
Eccremocarpus scaber. P. Climber.	Early spring for flower same year. 4°C (40°F).
Exacum affine. B.	March to June for flowering August to December. At least 10°C (50°F).
Freesia. P.	April to June. 7 months. 7°C (45°F).
Gerbera jamesonii. P.	March or when new seed available. 15 months for tall kinds but new compact hybrids flower same year. 10°C (50°F) for reliable winter flowering. (See p. 23.)
Gilia rubra. B.	Early spring for late summer and autumn or July to over-winter and flower next year. 7°C (45°F).
Grevillea robusta. P.	March. Foliage plant. 7°C (45°F). (See p. 48.)
Heliotropium peruvianum. P.	March. 15 weeks.
Hypoestes phyllostachya (*H. sanguinolenta*). P.	Foliage and house plant. 16°C (60°F). (See p. 40.)
Impatiens. A. and P, grown as A.	Spring in warmth. 11 weeks. 10°C (50°F).
Limonium suworowii. A.	Early spring for summer flowering.

Name	Sowing date; time taken to flower; MWT
Lobelia tenuior. A.	Spring for summer and summer for winter in cool greenhouse.
Nemesia strumosa. A.	March to June. 13 weeks. (See p. 40.)
Nierembergia hippomanica (N. caerulea) P.	March and April for late summer. Frost-free.
Pelargonium hybrids. P.	January on. 4 to 5 months according to temperature. 7°C (45°F).
Petunia. P, grown as A.	April. 14 weeks.
Plumbago auriculata (P. capensis). P. Climber.	Spring. 18 months. 4°C (40°F). (See p. 63.)
Primula vulgaris (modern hybrids) and *P. auricula.*	March to May. For winter and spring in unheated and frost-free greenhouse.
Primula x *kewensis, P. malacoides, P. obconica* and *P. sinensis.*	May to June for winter. 4°C (40°F). (See pp. 19 and 40.)
Punica granatum 'Nana' P.	Spring for autumn. Frost-free.
Rehmannia angulata. P.	May for following year. Frost-free.
Salpiglossis sinuata. A.	March and April. 20 weeks. Or August for May in slight heat. (See p. 40.)
Schizanthus pinnatus hybrids. A.	August for April and May, spring for summer. Frost-free. (See p. 6.)
Senecio x *hybridus.* B.	May to July for November to March. 7°C (45°F).
Streptocarpus. P.	February or March in warmth for midsummer. 10°C (50°F).
Thunbergia alata. A. Trailing or climber.	Late March. 15 weeks. (See p. 59.)
Torenia fournieri. A.	March and April. 15 weeks.
Trachelium caeruleum. P.	Early spring. 23 weeks. Or June for next year. 7°C (45°F).

Above: the polka dot plant, *Hypoestes phyllostachya* (left) needs warm
conditions; the brightly coloured nemesia (right) is a half-hardy annual
Below: modern forms of *Primula obconica* (left) come in
a wide range of colours; the striking salpiglossis (right) can be fully
appreciated in a greenhouse

Plants from cuttings

The greenhouse favourites grown from cuttings are in themselves enough to keep every greenhouse full of bloom all the year round, as well as providing a special hobby for a wide variety of people.

The actual process of taking cuttings has been revolutionised in recent years for the less skilled. Hormone rooting powders hasten rooting and make difficult species easier to strike, while the plastic bag has created a simple way of ensuring a moist environment for a potful of cuttings until rooting takes place. Mist propagation is a sophisticated option, but it is a luxury for those who do not need to raise many plants.

In general terms it is the vigorous young shoot, which has not yet reached the point of flowering or ripened its wood, that roots most readily. There are green tip cuttings, semi-ripe cuttings and hardwood cuttings, as well as leaf and root cuttings, but the favourite greenhouse plants in this chapter are increased by young shoots. These need to be neatly severed, with a sharp knife or razor blade, just beneath the node or joint and put into their rooting medium while still crisp and fresh.

The compost for cuttings should hold moisture yet drain freely, and there are many alternatives. A good formula is 1 part loam, 2 parts granulated peat and 3 parts coarse sand, all measured in bulk. Peat and sand in equal proportions is a much favoured mixture, while peat and sand, vermiculite or perlite are often used. Under mist pure sand is satisfactory, and it can be used without mist so long as it never dries. For cuttings that are not going to be potted up separately as soon as they have rooted, equal parts of loam, peat and sand provide more nutriment; and equal quantities of John Innes potting compost and sand is yet another alternative.

In any case the moisture of air and soil round the cuttings must never fail before they are rooted. Then they are gradually exposed to the air, first by opening and subsequently by removing the plastic bag or other covering.

In order to create enough plants for a group of ground cover in the garden, and for replacement of tender shrubs liable to be killed in a hard winter, some propagation is essential. Also, kind friends offer cuttings, for which unexpected gift the keen gardener is always ready with a plastic bag to take them home without wilting.

With perpetual-flowering carnations, removal of smaller side buds
results in quality blooms

A majority of greenhouse plants are propagated from cuttings,
and there are four favourites which for many are the principal
purpose and pleasure of a greenhouse.

Perpetual flowering carnations are still very popular with many
gardeners. The necessity here is to have healthy virus-free plants
and not to keep them for more than two years. There are specialist
nurserymen raising virus-free stock; they will often give advice to
the beginner. Little heat is needed, but plenty of air and good
winter light are essential. There needs to be room for the plants to
grow tall, and red spider must be effectively controlled. A
minimum winter temperature of 7°C (45°F) is desirable, as winter
is the principal flowering season and cut flowers the main
purpose. Cuttings can be rooted from November to March, and
spring is the time to buy rooted cuttings to start a collection.

Chrysanthemums are the favourite flower of countless enthusiasts in temperate climates, as well as a major horticultural
and artistic preoccupation in Japan. There is a good basis for such
universal acclaim, for not only is there a great variety of flower
size and type from which to choose but a spectacular response to
skilled cultivation and training. Chrysanthemums also brighten

the dark days of our autumn and early winter and provide exotic forms for flower arrangement.

Clearing out the greenhouse completely in summer and replacing the large plants with fresh young cuttings full of promise each spring are two aspects of chrysanthemum growing that appeal to many. Cuttings root at 7°C (45°C) and high temperatures are never needed. Healthy stock is important here too. (See also the Wisley Handbook, *Chrysanthemums and Dahlias*.)

The fuchsia is no less adaptable in the variety of ways in which it can be trained and grown and also responds to skill in cultivation. It naturally has a very long flowering season and cuttings strike easily at almost any time of year.

Where there is little heat or space, fuchsias can be overwintered by allowing them to become dormant in autumn, when watering is gradually reduced so that leaves fall and the wood ripens. They can take three to four months complete rest, but the root ball should be neither frozen nor dust dry during this time. They are then cut back and started into growth in February or

A Cascade chrysanthemum trained as a standard

March. Autumn cuttings, or young plants being grown as standards, have to be kept growing through the winter, for which a temperature of at least 7°C (45°F) is needed and 10°C (50°F) is preferred.

Again skill in cultivation brings great rewards. A poorly grown fuchsia is a poor thing indeed. A neutral or lime-free soil, and plenty of judicious feeding, and well-timed training are essential for real success. The plants are attractive to whitefly but otherwise trouble-free. A constant stream of new cultivars, as well as the very large selection of established varieties, means that there is an overwhelming choice. (See also the Wisley Handbook, *Fuchsias*.)

Perhaps the most universal favourite of the unskilled as well as the specialist is the geranium, more properly called the zonal pelargonium. The flow of new cultivars continues unabated, with special emphasis on dwarf, miniature and ivy-leaved kinds. The regal or show pelargoniums, flowering mainly from April to June, can be huge bushy plants with magnificent velvety flowers for the decoration of spacious places. Fortunately even more floriferous and adaptable dwarf regals have been created and there are a few miniatures. But all can be grown to a modest size, if confined to fairly small pots and renewed yearly from cuttings.

Zonal pelargoniums have been produced in such enormous numbers and brilliant colours for summer bedding, that not everyone realises the scope of the many kinds which, though they would not make a show in the open in one of our wet summers, are nevertheless good greenhouse and conservatory plants. A visit to a geranium nursery can be a revelation. There are even specialists in the miniature forms, and no greenhouse is too small to have a fascinating collection.

In recent years bedding geraniums that are raised from seed each year have been so much improved that they are often preferred for municipal bedding. These are usually raised in heat very early in the year and treated with hormone dwarfing agents to encourage early flowers and a better shape. The seed is costly and should have a temperature of 18°C (65°F) to germinate. They take much more water than the old geraniums and will not flower before July if conditions are poor. They respond well to automatic watering. All members of this family are very easily increased by cuttings, which need 7°C (45°F) to over-winter happily but survive much abuse.

As with so many plants constantly renewed from cuttings, there is much virus-infected stock, which is why seed-raised plants have become popular, otherwise they are healthy and long-suffering given sufficient ventilation and freedom from frost. The

Many pelargoniums have attractive foliage as well as flowers

danger of spreading virus infection has led the professionals to dispense with the knife when taking cuttings, but amateurs can use discarded razor blades or sterilise the knife between each cutting if there are only a few. Zonal pelargoniums are among the few cuttings best left uncovered for rooting, but as with all cuttings there must be shade from direct sunshine.

To produce a shapely pot plant with plenty of flowering shoots usually requires encouraging the early development of side shoots, and sometimes the prevention of flowering before maturity for the best results. (See also the Wisley Handbook, *Pelargoniums*.)

"Nip out the growing point at 6 in. (15cm) high" is a frequent instruction in horticulture and could be applied to any of the plants I have mentioned. However, so much thought has been given to the accurate timing of chrysanthemum blooms for show and to disbudding to increase their size, that any serious grower will follow a much more elaborate regime than I could detail here.

The training of woody pot plants is an art that has largely been lost in the last hundred years and can be learnt only by practice and example. In a small greenhouse or conservatory there would be room only for one or two elaborately trained specimen plants, and the emphasis must be on young plants and those that are naturally compact in growth.

45

Foliage plants

In the confined space of the small greenhouse all foliage is important. Even flowering plants with large coarse leaves are unlikely to be worth growing. No one should ignore foliage plants, for they are attractive all the year while many flowers only last a short time. They are helpful, too, in avoiding the flat effect of many small pot plants grown on one level, for there are trailers, trees, and palms, as well as the ferns and other shade lovers that grow happily under the staging. Flower arrangers will want trails of foliage to pick, while the strange forms of succulents are also effective in a mixed display. Some coloured leaves are as brilliant as any blossoms, and the cool greys and greens separate and enhance the brighter colours. In a conservatory one is particularly likely to want permanent plants in larger pots.

In the north facing or otherwise shaded greenhouse, plants grown for their foliage will be the mainstay, but even then the choice will be somewhat limited. It must be remembered that ferns need a damp atmosphere as well as shade. This is difficult to maintain in a small greenhouse or conservatory in summer even with artificial shading, if the structure is in a hot position.

The grey-white *Centaurea cineraria* (left) can be propagated annually from cuttings; the ivy-leaved pelargonium, 'L'Elegante' (right), is well named

The shining green leaves of *Kalanchoe blossfeldiana* are an added attraction to the colourful flowers

The foliage plants now grown as house plants enjoy warmth, but the glass will probably need shading from April to October. Most of them need a minimum winter temperature of at least 10°C (50°F) to do more than endure the winter, but all can be propagated and re-potted and generally encouraged to grow better, if there is a greenhouse available in the warmer months. The highly ornamental rex begonias and palms also appreciate shaded warmth in summer. The latter develop slowly and most will survive in the cool greenhouse or conservatory if gradually accustomed to cooler conditions.

Almost everyone seems to have a soft spot for grey leaves. Many such plants are valued in the garden but often lost in our wet winters, so that small plants over-wintered in the greenhouse may serve the double purpose of preserving the stock and providing a useful foil for the brighter colours.

The grey-leaved plants do not want warmth, only freedom from frost and not too rich a soil. The better forms of *Senecio cineraria* and *Centaurea cineraria* are well worth preserving and cuttings

47

can be rooted at the end of the summer. *Helichrysum petiolarum* is another decorative silver plant. *Tanacetum ptarmacaefolium* with silver leaves of a lacy fineness is raised from seed or cuttings. It is at its best in its second year if pruned in March.

Pelargoniums provide a number of coloured leaved and variegated plants. *Pelargonium graveolens* 'Lady Plymouth' with finely divided grey and white leaves is a favourite of mine. The cypress-like *P. crispum* 'Variegatum' with small crinkled cream and green foliage and the ivy leaf 'L'Elegante' that is green and white, and pink as well, if kept on the dry side, are other suggestions (see p. 46).

Amongst succulents, kalanchoes also provide a choice. *K. marmorata* has blue-grey leaves with brown freckles, while those of the plushy *K. tomentosa* are brown tipped. *Kalanchoe pumila* is a small grey-leaved plant for the front of the staging or a hanging basket. It has pink flowers in spring. These all thrive in 7°C (45°F) and are very easily renewed from cuttings (see pp. 25 and 47).

Asparagus fern is well known and there are several forms. *Asparagus densiflorus* 'Myers' with elegant plumes of foliage is an unusual plant to raise from seed and so is the pink spotted *Hypoestes phyllostachya* (*H. sanguinolenta*) (see p. 40).

For coloured leaves everyone knows *Coleus*, which can be rapidly grown from seed sown in spring or early summer. Other forms are raised from cuttings and can be grown into larger and finer specimens (see p. 10). In the warm greenhouse or conservatory codiaeums are no less colourful all the year round. Indeed in warmth the choice becomes very large with creepers and climbers, coloured veining and rich velvety surfaces.

Grevillea robusta is a fine foliage plant for a cool greenhouse

Bulbs, corms and tubers

Everyone loves bulbous plants in winter and early spring, and few of us fail to be impressed by the showy tuberous begonias or the cyclamen, hippeastrums and gloxinias in their season. Even the less widely grown but no less handsome *Haemanthus*, *Lachenalia*, *Nerine* and *Vallota* rouse the greatest enthusiasm when seen in flower. It is the dormant period of the bulbous plant that is its undoing. A bulb, tuber, corm or rhizome is a storage vessel, where the essentials for next year's flowering are kept safely until the favourable season for growth comes round again. Many of the most exotic bulbs from the southern hemisphere adapt fairly readily to a dry period of rest during our winters, instead of enduring a summer drought at home. However, under glass it is up to us to signal the changing seasons and it takes some foresight and an organised approach to grow the more tender bulbs successfully year after year.

Although generally speaking the spring flowering bulbs are planted or re-potted in autumn and the summer flowering ones are planted in spring, some fleshy rooted plants are never wholly dormant and others have a very brief rest, which does not fit in with the commercial arrangements for dry bulbs. For those who become interested in the more unusual bulbous plants, there is plenty to learn, quite apart from the possible thrills of travelling to see such plants in their native habitat. The serious collector of rare bulbs often has a bulb frame. This is a raised bed of freely draining soil, which can be protected from the rain or cold at the appropriate seasons for summer ripening or winter dormancy. Here the bulbs can be grouped according to seasonal behaviour and allowed to grow naturally. This method does not create a show of bloom at any one time, but it does allow the best development of the smaller rarer bulbs, the habits of which are sometimes little known. Every bulb has its preferred position in the soil and most will adjust themselves to their natural depth in time, no matter how they are planted.

Although the idea of raising bulbous plants from seed is usually rejected by the beginner, it is not necessarily a slow process. The beautiful *Lilium formosanum* can be flowered in nine months; freesias flower in seven months from a spring sowing and are very easy to grow. The fifteen or sixteen months it can take to

Lachenalia aloides (left) and *Veltheimia bracteata* (right), two unusual bulbous plants for the cool greenhouse

raise a hybrid cyclamen from seed is more exacting, but some of the smaller newer hybrids are very much quicker (see p. 21).

The problem of how to rest a cyclamen corm always provokes conflicting advice, which only goes to show how adaptable fleshy rooted plants are to any steady regime. The secret is to keep them dry but not totally dry, from when the leaves start yellowing until that awkward moment when everyone is on holiday in August and the cyclamen is ready to be re-potted. Do not worry; leave it in the shade outside the back door where the rain will reach it, and you will be reminded to re-pot it on your return.

The small hardy wild cyclamen species, sometimes grown in pans in the unheated greenhouse, can be difficult to start into growth when bought dry and may remain dormant for a year.

Begonias have tiny seeds and need warmth from the time they are sown in January, and it is less demanding to grow them from tubers in spring (see p. 30). The same is true of gloxinias. If they are to be enjoyed again the following year, they must be dried off gradually in October, so that the fleshy roots ripen and the foliage dries off completely before they are stored. They can remain in their pots or be put in dry peat and kept frost free, preferably at a temperature around 10°C (50°F). They are started into growth again in March.

In an unheated greenhouse only the hardy bulbs can be grown in winter, but they will flower several weeks earlier than those in the open. Amongst the smaller hardy bulbs that are attractive in pots in January are the early crocus species and *Iris histrioides* 'Major', followed by the yellow *I. danfordiae* and the scented *I. reticulata* (see p. 31). Another of my favourites is the scarlet multi-flowered *Tulipa praestans*.

'Pink Pearl' (left) is a long-established hyacinth cultivar; the half-hardy *Tigridia pavonia* (right) flowers in early summer

Vallota speciosa is an evergreen bulbous plant that is shy-flowering until pot-bound and may be difficult to start if sold as a dry bulb. The big scarlet flowers in late summer are worth having. Another evergreen with fleshy roots is *Clivia miniata* and this too can remain in the same pot for years. Its handsome orange or yellow flowers usually appear in late spring.

Perhaps the most spectacular of all glasshouse bulbs are the *Hippeastrum* hybrids (often wrongly called *Amaryllis*) that produce the largest flowers in scarlet, white, pink or orange, to silence the most querulous visitor. They often manage two spikes of four flowers each, although they occasionally miss a year and lose friends that way. Early spring is the planting time, except for those specially prepared for Christmas flowering, which will join the others in blooming in April and May in subsequent years. They need to be gradually induced to rest in September, until they show signs of life in spring. Some obstinately remain evergreen and all need 10°C (50°F) in winter when developing flowers, but are quite happy in cooler conditions once in bloom (see p. 32).

Other fleshy rooted flowering plants to try in the warmer greenhouse or conservatory are *Achimenes*, *Gesneria*, *Gloriosa*, *Haemanthus* and *Smithiantha* (see p. 56). Suggestions for cooler conditions include the winter flowering *Lachenalia*, hybrid nerines flowering in autumn and the handsome *Veltheimia*, which are ornamental through the winter and flower in spring. In an unheated or just frost-free greenhouse, the nearly hardy bulbous plants sometimes grown outdoors are worth considering. These include *Agapanthus*, *Ixia*, *Nerine bowdenii* (see p. 9), *Sparaxis*, *Streptanthera* and *Tigridia*. (See also the Wisley Handbook, *Growing Dwarf Bulbs*.)

Climbers and shrubs

There is no distinct division between climbers and trailers under glass, or indeed between climbers and shrubs if the latter can be persuaded to cover a wall. In a conservatory climbers give a furnished look and may also be used to give shade. The passion flower (*Passiflora caerulea*) is particularly useful (see p. 63). All climbers and shrubs planted in the ground under glass will have to endure frequent and severe pruning, if they are not to overwhelm the place quite soon.

In a small structure space is so important that one must either confine the roots in a pot or tub or limit oneself to one climber trained up to the roof or back wall. All the favourite conservatory plants are inclined to be rampant. The passion flower can be confined to a tub for a time and pruned hard back in winter. The same is true of the sweet-scented *Jasminum polyanthum* that will root at every joint and grow twelve foot in a season, although young plants blooming in a 5-inch pot look innocent enough. The pale blue *Plumbago auriculata* (*P. capensis*) is a big sprawling shrub with a long flowering season. It is quick and easy from seed or cuttings, takes hard pruning and will even submit to a pot, but cannot really do itself justice that way. There is also a white flowered form (see p. 63).

The Australian blue bell creeper (*Sollya fusiformis*) also has pale blue flowers and grows quickly from seed, but is of modest proportions. The beautiful *Lapageria rosea*, the national flower of Chile, must have a lime-free soil. It is evergreen with small neat leaves, and is slow-growing when confined to a pot. It likes shady cool conditions and the rosy pendant flowers are striking.

There is much to be said for a modest climber that dies back and makes a fresh growth from the root each year. Nature has limited its scope and you do not have to harden your heart and chop it down. *Gloriosa superba* and particularly *G. rothschildiana* is always greatly admired and may reach 6 ft (1.8m), but is a dry root for half the year (see p. 2).

Tropaeolum tricolorum from Chile is a tuberous rooted climber of moderate vigour that dies down in mid-summer and rests until growth starts again. Light support will be needed for the twining growths wreathed with scarlet and black flowers in spring.

Morning glory (*Ipomoea*) and *Eccremocarpus scaber* are two climbers which are easily raised from seed and come quickly into flower.

The spectacular *Lapageria rosea* carries bell-shaped flowers in summer and autumn

Fuchsias have been mentioned in other chapters and can be trained to any shape, but *F. procumbens* from New Zealand is a curious trailing plant for pots that few would recognise as a fuchsia. The yellow and purple flowers are followed by red berries.

Those with a wall in a sunny conservatory may be attracted by bougainvilleas (see p. 59). If happy, they ramp with thorny branches, but if unhappy they may forget to flower and be covered with greenfly. Plants as diverse as *Begonia fuchsioides* and zonal pelargoniums can be trained against a wall, and the important thing is to choose a plant that is not too attractive to pests. One of these, the orange flowered *Streptosolen jamesonii*, is an amenable bush for training upwards, and its hanging flowers look their best from below (see p. 33).

A group of climbers that are not too thrusting in a small space are the hoyas. Their clustered blossoms look more like wax or icing sugar than any form of plant life. *Hoya bella* is a tricky but beautiful basket plant for the warm greenhouse and *H. carnosa* a less demanding climber in a pot in cool conditions.

Small shrubs in pots often arrive as gifts, such as the Christmas azaleas, and it becomes a matter of pride to keep them from year to year. Plunged outdoors in light shade from June to October and re-potted if necessary in April, they can be kept going for years by those who manage never to forget to water them. They should

53

have 7°C (45°F) and a moist atmosphere to bring on the bloom.

The modern poinsettia (*Euphorbia pulcherrima*) is less demanding than its forebears, but prefers a temperature of 13°C (55°F) and regular watering. After a dry and cooler rest in summer, it can be kept for another year, being pruned and re-potted when growth starts naturally. It will flower later and the bracts may be smaller, but they are invariably more plentiful.

Hibiscus rosa-sinensis is now a popular house plant that flowers for months but needs 13°C (55°F) in winter.

Camellias are irresistible in flower and valuable in a north facing cool or cold conservatory. They are best outside in summer as they are hardy plants only needing protection for their winter flowers. (See also the Wisley handbook, *Camellias*.)

For spring the mimosa best suited in size and slowness of growth to a confined space is *Acacia armata*, with narrow stems of small leaves dotted with little mimosa puffs (see p. 10). The dwarf pomegranate *Punica granatum* 'Nanum' quickly grown from seed to flower at 3 in. (7.5cm) tall is the nearest thing to a mini shrub designed for the beginner in a mini greenhouse.

Camellias are very successful in a cold or cool greenhouse

Specialisation

In earlier chapters I have mentioned some of the favourite flowering plants that often capture the whole attention of amateurs. Perpetual flowering carnations, chrysanthemums, fuchsias and the various pelargoniums are all attractive plants with long flowering seasons that respond well to skilled cultivation. Each one of them can become an absorbing hobby. Many people find it more satisfying to know a great deal about a limited subject than to have a smattering of knowledge over a wide field and it is always worth joining a specialist society.

One way of specialising is in groups of related plants. The gesneriads are an interesting family that have become more freely available in recent years. The saintpaulia or African violet started the craze, as it is so widely grown as a house plant, but it is not generally successful in a mixed collection of plants. It needs a warm greenhouse to be happy, as do *Aescynanthus, Columnea, Episcia,* and *Smithiantha. Streptocarpus* has free flowering and relatively tolerant hybrids seen both in the cool greenhouse and on the window sill and there are also strange and interesting species. Some gesneriads have underground storage organs that are dormant in winter and can be grown in any greenhouse in summer. *Achimenes,* gloxinia (*Sinningia*), *Kohleria* and *Rechsteineria* are the best known.

Most people either love or hate the cactus family, but enough are interested to support a very active national society and countless local groups. Today there is no need or excuse for growing plants imported from native habitats, many of which have been devastated by commercial exploitation. Specialist growers in Britain and elsewhere can supply an infinite variety of nursery-grown plants, while enthusiasts also exchange seed and plants amongst themselves.

Those who decide to specialise in cacti, rare succulents, or the wild species of orchids should be particularly vigilant about the sources of their plants and the need not to decimate their original habitat. Although the individual can do little to safeguard a threatened species, every person who unthinkingly buys plants collected in the wild is encouraging this destructive trade.

(For further information, see the Wisley Handbooks, *Begonias, Bromeliads, Cacti, Carnivorous Plants, Houseplants, Orchids* and *Succulents.*)

Above: the foxglove-like flowers of *Smithiantha* make their appearance in summer and autumn
Below: Cascade chrysanthemums require specialist treatment and training but this does not deter enthusiasts

Pests and diseases

No matter what views one may hold about pests and diseases or poison sprays, the golden rule under glass is to start clean. With the new greenhouse there is no problem, but in the year-round warmth of heated greenhouses there is bound to be a gradual build up of unwanted guests unless preventive steps are taken. Some may be engaged in eating others and there is much talk of preserving beneficial predators and parasites. All the same, the owners of small greenhouses are less concerned with the rights and wrongs of insects or the arguments for or against chemical and biological control than with easy remedies.

We want to prevent pests or diseases from consuming or disfiguring our plants and to do so without endangering ourselves or our children. This is not as simple as it sounds, because some of the most damaging insects gradually become resistant to remedies that are regularly applied. Varying the chemicals used prevents a build-up of pest resistance.

Our first thought must always be to avoid introducing pests or diseases into the greenhouse. It is worth being quite ruthless about this. Every plant needs the most careful examination before being added to a collection. The soft growing points and the undersides of the leaves are the places to look. This may sound fussy, but two weeks isolation followed by another close examination is even more effective. If in doubt spray with pesticide.

Some pests will always be with us, unless we are willing to have a continuous discharge of some chemical or a frequent and regular spraying or fumigation in the greenhouse. Personally I would rather keep a sharp look out and spray only actual enemies when seen.

PESTS

There are five extremely persistent greenhouse pests that one needs to keep under control, and recognition of these is essential. These are vine weevil, mealybugs, red spider mites, whitefly and aphids.

Vine weevil. The adult beetles are $\frac{3}{8}$ in. (8–9 mm) long and dull black with tiny yellow-brown patches on their wing cases. They are active at night when they eat notches from the leaf margins of many plants. The larval stage is more important as it feeds on the roots and corms of most pot plants and often kills them. The larvae are white, legless grubs up to ⅜ in. (10 mm) long, with pale brown heads. The adults are mainly present in late spring and early summer but may be found at any time between March and November. Torchlight inspections can be useful for finding and destroying the adults when signs of leaf damage are seen. The grubs are harder to control, especially when almost fully grown. Some protection against young larvae can be given by drenching the compost with spray strength pirimiphos-methyl or HCH in early July and early August. Biological control, in the form of a nemotode drench, is becoming available. Good results can be achieved by treating pot plants in late summer before the larvae have grown large enough to cause damage.

Mealybugs. These creatures which look like tiny white woodlice are clearly visible to those with normal sight, and their presence is usually first noticed as a small patch of white wool, which means they are breeding. Fortunately they do not spread rapidly in the early stages, but they are hard to kill. Picking off each insect with a pin or painting them and their eggs with methylated spirits are two effective methods for small infestation. This pest is the only major pest of cacti and succulents and can spread to other plants.

In heavier infestations, pirimiphos-methyl, malathion or one of the systemic insecticides, such as dimethoate, may be used either as sprays or, in the case of the systemics, as soil drenches.

Red spider mites. These are serious pests, particularly as the early stages are hard to spot, since the individual mites can barely be seen. Affected leaves become pallid due to the thousands of bleached spots where the mites are feeding on the under surface. The mites are straw-coloured, turning in autumn to minute red spider-like creatures that can clearly be seen with a hand lens, weaving webs over the lower surfaces of the leaves. This pest revels in a hot dry atmosphere and spraying the under surfaces of the leaves of woody plants with water in warm weather helps to prevent trouble. The plants most likely to be attacked are shrubs and carnations, but almost all greenhouse plants are susceptible.

Red spider mites quickly become resistant to any chemical that is used regularly but some reduction of infestations may be obtained by spraying thoroughly with derris, pirimiphos-methyl, malathion or dimethoate. Alternatively, biological control may be attempted during the summer by introducing the red spider mite predator, *Phytoseiulus persimilis* (for suppliers see p. 62).

Glasshouse whitefly. These are tiny snow-white insects that rise into the air when the plants are disturbed. Both adults and their

Thunbergia gregorii (left) resembles *T. alata*, but does not have the "black eye"; *Bougainvillea glabra* and its forms (right) are the best choice for a cool greenhouse, flowering when quite small

nymphs are sucking insects with a complicated life cycle and all remedies have to be applied several times to eradicate this persistent pest. Many plants are affected including regal pelargoniums, fuchsias, cucumber, tomato and poinsettia.

Whitefly can be controlled by spraying or fumigating the plants with permethrin. This is a persistent but safe chemical that can be used on a wide range of plants, including tomatoes and cucumbers. Less persistent alternatives are insecticidal soaps, bioresmethrin, pyrethrum, HCH, malathion and pirimiphos-methyl. In some areas there are strains of whitefly that have gained resistance to some of these insecticides. Yellow sticky traps can help reduce infestations, particularly if plants are regularly shaken to encourage the adult whitefly to fly.

Biological control may be attempted using a parasite, *Encarsia formosa*, but it only operates effectively when daytime temperatures are above 21°C (70°F).

Aphids. Various forms of greenfly, which may also be black, buff or pink, are certain to appear. Many are killed by any kind of pesticide, but unfortunately some have developed resistance to certain chemicals. I try pyrethrum or derris and more toxic alternatives. Fully and partially systemic insecticides such as dimethoate, heptenophos and pirimicarb are absorbed into the plant's sap and kill the aphids as they feed. As with all insecticides, the manufacturer's instructions regarding the interval required between spraying and harvesting must be observed if these insecticides are used on food plants. In summer various forms of hoverfly take a high toll of greenfly and should never be discouraged.

Ants. Ants transport aphids from plant to plant and thereby spread virus diseases as well as pests. For this reason they must be discouraged from establishing themselves in the greenhouse.

HCH dusts or proprietary ant baits may be used in areas where they are troublesome, and these control measures should be applied in and around the nesting sites rather than on plants which ants are visiting.

Slugs. These feed mainly at night and make holes in leaves, flowers and stems. Seedlings and cuttings can be severely checked. Scatter slug pellets around affected plants.

Leafhoppers. The adults are ⅛ in. (2–3 mm) long and pale yellow with darker markings. They readily jump off the leaf when disturbed, so it is often easier to find the less mobile, creamy white, immature nymphs. Both stages suck sap from the lower leaf surface, causing a coarse whitish green mottling of the upper leaf surface. Many plants are affected. Leafhoppers are controlled by the chemicals listed under red spider mite.

Leaf-miners. Chrysanthemums and related plants such as cineraria, gazania and senecio are often attacked by the larvae of a leaf-mining fly. They make twisting linear tunnels in the leaves and spoil the plant's appearance. Removing affected parts of the leaves can prevent damage if the infestation is caught early enough, otherwise spray with pirimiphos-methyl or HCH. Use only the latter on cineraria.

Earwigs. It is in hot dry summers that earwigs often cause mysterious punctured holes to appear in the leaves of succulents and they also damage chrysanthemum and other flowers.

They can be trapped under old sacking and seed-boxes or in flower pots stuffed with straw or similar materials. HCH dust applied to their hiding places also reduces numbers.

Scales. The protective coverings of scale insects are sometimes found on the backs of the leaves of oleanders and other evergreens. From this safe hiding place they suck the sap of a wide range of plants.

Thorough spraying of the undersides of leaves with malathion or pirimphos-methyl in spring and summer will check infestations, and small pot plants can be hand cleaned using soft rags dipped in soapy water.

Thrips. Thrips are minute blackish grey, winged insects that are

A mixture of begonias, fuchsias and schizanthus gives a brilliant show

hard to find, but the damage they cause is rather similar to that of red spider. They will not become established unless the atmosphere is too dry and spraying with clear water discourages them. If an insecticide is necessary, they can be controlled by spraying with malathion, derris or HCH.

Sciarid flies or fungus gnats. These are greyish brown flies, $\frac{3}{16}$ in. (3–4 mm) long, that run over the compost or fly slowly around pot plants. They do not feed so are a nuisance rather than a pest. Their larvae are thin white maggots with black heads. They live in the compost where they feed on decaying organic material such as dead roots. They sometimes damage living roots on seedlings and cuttings but will not harm healthy established plants. Fumigation with HCH or permethrin will reduce the adult flies if they are too numerous, as will the use of sticky yellow traps. Protect vulnerable plants from the grubs by mixing malathion dust with the compost, or water with spray strength HCH or pirimiphos-methyl.

61

Springtails. When watering pot plants, white insects about 1 mm long are often seen crawling or hopping on the soil surface or in the drainage saucer. These springtails are entirely harmless as they feed on decaying organic matter in the compost, and so control measures are not required.

Suppliers of biological controls:
English Woodlands Ltd., Graffham, Petworth, Sussex GU28 0LR

Henry Doubleday Research Association, Ryton Court, Wolston Lane, Ryton on Dunsmore, Coventry CV8 3L

Natural Pest Control (Amateur), Watermead, Yapton Road, Barnham, Bognor Regis, West Sussex, PO2 0BQ

Applied Horticulture, Fargro Ltd, Toddington Lane, Littlehampton, West Sussex BN17 7PP

All of the above supply *Encarsia* and *Phytoseiulus*; Applied Horticulture also supply the vine weevil control.

DISEASES

Damping-off. This disease is caused by several different soil and water-borne fungi which cause the collapse of seedlings at ground level. It is most troublesome where seedlings are overcrowded, overwatered, grown in unsterilized compost or watered with non-mains water. Prevent infection by sowing seeds in sterilized compost and by watering carefully with mains water.

Foot rot, crown rot and root rot. These may be caused by the same fungi as those causing damping-off and also by others. A brown or black rot of the tissues at the base of the stems, around the crowns or at the roots results in wilting or collapse of the top growth. Use sterilized compost and pots and clean water to prevent infection. It is sometimes possible to save a diseased plant by watering with a solution of a copper fungicide.

Grey mould (Botrytis cinerea). This fungus causes rotting of leaves, stems and flowers, the affected tissues becoming covered with a grey-brown mass of fungal spores. In less severe cases small red or brown spots develop on petals. The disease is most troublesome in greenhouses where the humidity is high and hygiene is poor. Prevent infection by the prompt removal and burning of all diseased or dying parts. Ventilate well to reduce the humidity and water early in the morning and not at night. Fumigate with tecnazene smokes, or spray with carbendazim, benomyl or thiophanate-methyl at the first signs of the disease.

The passion flower, *Passiflora caerulea* (left), a reliable and almost hardy climber; *Plumbago auriculata* (right) can be hard pruned in late winter

Powdery mildew. This type of disease shows as a white powdery coating on the leaves and sometimes the flowers and the stems of chrysanthemums, begonias, cinerarias and occasionally other plants. As the fungi are encouraged by humid atmospheres ventilate the greenhouse well. Plants that are dry at the roots are more susceptible to infection so water before the compost dries out completely. Remove severely affected leaves and spray with benomyl, carbendazim, propiconazole, fenarimol, thiophanate-methyl or triforine.

Rusts. The rusts of fuchsias and cineraria show as orange powdery pustules on the lower leaf surfaces, but on chrysanthemums, pelargoniums and carnations the pustules produce masses of chocolate-coloured spores. Remove and burn affected leaves and in severe cases destroy the whole plant. Ventilate the greenhouse well to reduce the humidity, and when watering, make sure that droplets do not remain on the leaves. Spray at seven to ten-day intervals with mancozeb, propiconazole, thiram or triforine. For fuchsias the only suitable fungicide is mancozeb as the others are likely to cause phytotoxic damage.

Viruses. Cucumber mosaic and other viruses can affect a wide range of plants causing mottling, botching or striping of the leaves, the affected parts being pale green, yellow or black. The leaves may also be distorted and the plants stunted. Destroy any plant showing these symptoms. Control aphids by suitable spraying as these pests transmit some viruses including cucumber mosaic.

Physiological disorders. These are due to unsuitable cultural conditions and are very common on greenhouse plants. The commonest disorder is called oedema and in this the plant shows pale pimple-like outgrowths on the undersurface of the leaves and on the stems. Later they burst and become brown and powdery or corky. Ivy-leaved pelargoniums are particularly susceptible to this trouble which is due to overwatering and/or too humid an atmosphere. Improve the cultural conditions by careful watering and ventilation. Do not remove affected leaves.

Bud drop. The dropping or withering of buds is usually due to drying out of the compost at a critical stage of growth. Do not allow the compost to dry out when flower buds are just beginning to develop.

*Corky scab.*This shows on cacti as irregular rusty or corky spots which develop into sunken patches. This is due to lack of light and too high humidity or over-exposure to sunlight. Where the trouble is very unsightly propagate from the affected plant and give the new plants correct cultural treatment.

As temperatures fall in the autumn it becomes especially important to remove dead flowers and foliage and to avoid a damp and stuffy atmosphere. Moulds develop most easily on decayed vegetation, but flowers and soft growth may be spoiled by the dreaded grey mould (see above) if there is not heat or ventilation to keep the air moving.

For those who do not use a greenhouse in winter this is the time to take out and burn all those plant remains, while the rest of us make the hard decisions as to what to save and what to propagate for another year. By late September we need to be ready for a hard frost with all tender plants under cover, the heating system tested, and fuel in store. For the real greenhouse enthusiast there are flowers for every season and the warmer the greenhouse the earlier the spring.